Between Chaos And Calm

Ritika Pagaria

BookLeaf Publishing

India | USA | UK

Made with ❤ on the BookLeaf Publishing Platform
www.bookleafpub.in
www.bookleafpub.com

Dedication

For those who wonder if their voice is strong enough, if their light shines bright enough, or if their actions will matter—this is for you. Don't let doubt dim your gifts. Your words, your art, your heart have the power to change the world in ways you may never fully see. Keep creating, keep believing, and never let the fear of 'not enough' stop you from shining.

Preface

Welcome to this concoction of mine, where words swirl together like unexpected ingredients in a pot, each poem a different flavor, each thought a different spice, blending to create a complex bouquet of emotions and ideas. This collection has been a journey of discovery, a series of meandering paths through memory, nature, and the hidden corners of the soul.

Some poems are like unexpected lottery wins—gems that appear when least expected, like *Unexpected Windfall*, where a diamond and friendship intertwine in an exploration of chance and connection. Others are like the quiet reverie of old gardens and lost moments, much like *Garden Reminiscence*, where the scent of nostalgia fills the air with a bittersweet sense of time passed.

Through these pages, I've wrestled with the quiet beauty of a sunrise, the fading glow of sunset, and the mystery of nature's mask—the way beauty often wears a cloak, hiding its true form beneath. There are poems about the library's hallowed halls, the labyrinth of time, and the small but profound wonder in every corner of life.

And just as each poem feels like its own journey, this

collection is a map of mine, sketched out in the margins of my days. The process of creation was like brewing a broth from the oddest of ingredients—thoughts, emotions, experiences—some bitter, some sweet, and all woven together with the quiet hope that the flavor would become something beautiful.

Now, dear reader, you are the taste tester. Sip as I did—savor the unexpected bursts of flavor, the subtle notes that linger long after the page is turned. Take a ride with me through these verses. The path may twist and turn, but I hope you find something that resonates, something that echoes your own experiences or takes you to a place you've never been before.

So here it is: my soup of words, mixed with all the passion and whimsy I could muster. May you find joy in these pages as I found in creating them.

Acknowledgements

First, a massive thank you to my parents for being my unwavering support system throughout this journey. From countless hours of encouragement to their patient faces as I rambled on about metaphors and wordplay, you've always had my back. A heartfelt shout-out to my younger brother and sister for being my ultimate cheerleaders, even when my poetry had them wondering if I was secretly plotting a revolution.

To my dear uncle and aunties, your wisdom, laughter, and kindness have shaped me in countless ways. I am also deeply thankful for my grandparents, whose strength, stories, and timeless values have instilled in me a sense of purpose and connection.

To all my teachers - thank you for showing me that "playing with words" could be more than just a hobby. Special thanks to Mrs. Pierce, who not only believed in my "talent" (and I use that term loosely) but also published my work in the school newsletter. And Mrs. Vagnoni, you're the reason I'm here—and yes, I do credit you for my slight obsession with words.

A huge thanks to my classmates for reading, reviewing,

or just lending a listening ear. And to my friends
sprinkled among them, thank you for making me feel
like my rhyming obsession was worth it. If I missed
anyone, you know who you are—your support has meant
the world to me, even if I didn't name you.

Finally, to the readers—this book would be nothing
without you. You've made this journey meaningful and
life changing. Thank you for your encouragement,
curiosity, and simply for being here. This book exists
because of you, and for that, I'm forever grateful.

War and Peace

War is conflict, deep inside
Viewed through vexed and fuming eyes
War is battle within thyself
To soothing words, thy heart is deaf.

War is that which sneaks up on the brave
The thirsty lords who arrogance crave
Be wary of devious, intruding thoughts
Slithering words fetch bloodshed ought.

War is a force not to be reckoned
Unless thou yearns for carnage beckoned
Heed thy numerous warnings bestowed
Or else lives shall be lost, and blood tearfully sowed.

Peace is the fragile calm after the storm
The restless wait for the inevitable more
The fleeting moment thou grows to cherish
Grasping, though it shall eventually perish.

Peace is serenity, a temporary truce
Composure and placidity, thou shall induce
Hold on to thy children, milk all of life's worth
The deepest secrets, thou shall unearth.

Blink back the past and live in the moment
Leave it to fate for imminent bestowment
Be it life or death, ecstasy or sorrow
Fret about today, never tomorrow.

Tis' but how the world runs by
Violence chasing ease across the sky
Destiny consoles yet takes back, as it must
Generous to ye—not fair, but just.

One Little Smile

When spirit falls low and the mood is depressed,
When bliss slips away, leaving you feeling suppressed,
When it seems that you've lost that spark of connection,
Look for the light in the smallest reflection.

One move, like trading smiles with a friend forlorn,
Can soften the sorrow and joy adorn
Like stars sparkling in the shadows of night,
For one little smile can leave you reeling in delight.

Tell me, who started this cycle of reaction,
Was it you or just another's dissatisfaction?
Stop the chain before it starts, my friend,
Halt the tide before it sweeps you again.

Yes, it will try, but resist the urge to fight,
Don't confuse productive outlets with stifled spite.
Release the tension, feel lighter once more,
For one little smile can heal what was sore.

So, speak a kind word to the quiet, the withdrawn,
Even a small gesture can help bring the start of dawn,
Beat back the murkiness, piece by piece,
Oh, the boiling tension, gratefully release.

In the discreet moments when shadows may fall,
Remember the power we each have to call
A brighter tomorrow, with words softly spoken,
For one little smile can help without any need for a
token.

Silence, Deafening Silence

Silence, deafening silence
Abrupt pauses laced with tension
Silence, deafening silence
The standstill after confrontation.
Silence, deafening silence
A void ripping emotion astray
Oh, silence, posing as
The storm's premature display.

Silence, prophetic silence
The sinking sensation that feels possessed
Silence, prophetic silence
Clashing gallantry strangely repressed
Silence, prophetic silence
Fierce, bane of the haughty turned gray
Oh, silence, deceptively soft—
Like a wolf stalking its hard-earned prey.

Silence, careful silence
May be woven by threads of compliance

But silence, daunting silence
Is concocted of powerful strings of defiance.

Beacon of Hope

Hope is plain prophecy
A sign of what is to appear
The twilight zone of the morning
The sun's gorgeous premiere.
To sworn enemy despair's leeching
Tries to resiliently interfere
Succeeds when the shadows seem
To all lost souls adhere.

With allusions of hearth abandoned
Only hope and gloom are to be found
Fully anchor your heart to belief
Keep it growing and profound.
Let go of the murkiness so black
Creeping in from all around
For in the art of divination
Hope's the best seer renowned.

Carrier of good times come forth
Let it guide the adrift souls to shore

Lend a line to those sinking ships
Proud and certain beings restore.
Beat back the despondency looming
So achingly threatening war
For now, the light has come to cut through the dark
No misery left anymore.

Nature's Mask

Rustling underbrush, thriving and serene
Wonders of nature, wild and green
Colors that pop, vivid and strong
Exotic fragrances that strangely belong.

Vibrant flowers you won't believe
Taken for granted though all perceive
Wouldn't doubt the bliss at first look, you see
Slinking illusions speak of partial reality.

Behind the trees, tall and proud
Huddle the aging flowers in the darkened shroud
Losing the battle for light, they fade
Into mere ghosts where hope has decayed.

Nature's mask hides what we dread to face
Veracity it veils, like silhouettes in space
Though it doesn't mean that beauty isn't real
Simply that façades have backsides they conceal.

Mother Earth spoils us, giving us green
Suppressing greys that we haven't seen
Though behind the shallowness lies a depth extreme
While maintaining others' high esteem.

Those who search will find the fact
Secreted behind veils of tact
Poison behind hues sickeningly bright
We know to avoid because of our instincts alight.

Yet in this dance of light and dark
Where splendor thrives and shadows hark
We, too, wear masks, blind to what's concealed
Chasing beauty's glow while shadows are revealed.

Nature's mask will always remain
A paradox we cannot explain
But in its depths, we learn to see
The world's raw heart, wild and free.

Wonders of Time

Dainty hands moving steadily by,
Chimes echoing across the world awry,
An ageless force none can deny,
Flat arms against the number-stitched sky.

A force of nature, influential and strong,
Endless faces will imminently throng,
Its rigid hand just strings the living along,
For none escape what time can prolong.

A certain amount of joy and sorrow,
A fleeting gift to be returned by tomorrow.
Grants us the night for a quick little borrow,
Then asks it back with the view in morrow.

Time moves slow when the stillness calls,
While fleeting moments softly fall.
Intricate fingers, they glide through all,
For majestic time, none can forestall.

Promise of Sunset

The beginning of the sun's descent
Cut into a neat arch across the sky,
Colorful rays putting on a light show
From their sinking source far west.
The lit beams gracefully encompass
The orb-shaped heavens above,
Laced with shimmering clouds like thin strings
Weaving the tapestry of life.
Some say the sun has given up,
While others claim it was never there—
They fail to understand that in the darkest hours,
It cannot solve everything.
Sometimes light isn't enough,
And the sun knows this truth:
It allows the darkness to take over,
Offering solace in the quiet of dusk.
We know it's only taking a break,
A brief escape to the other side,
Waiting for the perfect moment
To rise, once again, after the long night.

Fulfillment of Sunrise

Sweet summer-scented sky
Dawn stretching over the horizon
Crisp air heavy with the morning breeze
Tickling bare arms spread wide with awe.
Twilight flooding the world with colors anew
Creeping across the sky from west to east
Clouds unveiling to reveal the sun
In all its mystic glory.
Melodic chirping filling the brief silence
Yawns heard over the land's wide expanse
Specks of light dancing on the flowers
Patiently waiting to be fed.
At last, light has graced the land
Elegant and sprawling, like the ruler of the heavens
Rays alight signaling the majestic start to a new day.
Shimmering stars blinking out of sight
Promising that they'll be back
Twinkling mysteriously, like indulging in goodbye
At least until the sun has completed its shift.

Where Worlds Meet

Where erudition's native soil resides
Musty paper, where intellect presides
A building made of much more than halls
The library, where the fourth wall falls.

Inside, they say you can sail the seven seas
Play Sherlock Holmes, solve mysteries
History known in no more than a sitting
Magic worker, truly befitting.

Tragic tales born from scattered emotion anew
Make you feel every color, every shade, every hue
Made from gold dust, no less precious, each word a light
A beacon for the soul, shining brightly through the
night.

From deities, once proud, shown their place in life
To stories of sorrow, loss, and bitter strife
Yet in these pages, healing softly grows
A refuge for the heart, where light softly glows.

Most avoid the "stress" because of conventions
Say they have enough with school and pretensions
Yet the hearth burning in my chest begs to negate
The assumptions that others recklessly make.

In whispered silence, knowledge hums and flows,
A timeless refuge where the curious grows.
No boundless thought, no dream, no quest is lost,
For in the library, all worlds meet, no matter the cost.

Garden Reminiscence

I fell back into the long grass,
Untrimmed and itchy yet such a relief,
Smelt the delicate roses made of glass,
Tried to brush away the incoming disbelief.

Did I have to move away from my old home so dear,
The treehouse I'd made my own through bribes,
The beloved town that felt frontier—
Comfy and cozy, with all the best vibes.

A lone tear slipped out of my eyes, incredulous,
At the remarkably sudden change of scenery,
Away from my older sis, admittedly querulous,
Yet the only one who shared my interest in greenery.

I sniffled sadly, turning on my side,
Gently reached out and brushed the pansies,
Held back tears and nearly cried,
At the fragile flowers she said she fancies.

I miss my sister and the friendships I fostered,
The crooked tree that gave us shade,
The creeping vines that surprisingly prospered,
But most of all, my home which *they* would soon invade.

I frowned at that cheery note, slumping against the
ground,
Then sat up and unraveled my barely muddied hair,
And despite my reluctance to leave the garden profound,
Decided to depart and bury my despair.

As I passed the fence, I felt a firm breeze,
Carrying a stray petal from a rose strewn about,
A smile danced on my lips, undoubtedly pleased,
Because this had to be a sign from nature's route.

Unexpected Windfall

I'd been floating past the gardens lush
Feet scarcely touching the earth
The serenity unbroken, the gentle hush
Felt like I had gracefully rebirth.

A sharp prick in my foot set me back
Stumbling two steps before stopping
A stone nestled in a jagged crack
Had me on my toes and dropping.

Dug out a marble-sized crystal with blood smeared
across it
An iridescent diamond behind the crimson red
With a bit of care, I'd be able to gloss it
And make it a true jewel with a shining head.

An hour passed and the sun started to sink
Lit rays bounced off the sparkling top
Prismatic colors hovered, and there sounded a *clink!*
As I let go of the gem I'd been holding nonstop.

Finally, I stepped back and observed my find
Hit the jackpot, hadn't I today?
A diamond, with clever features defined
Brilliant luck, as my parents would say.

But then came *him*, my new neighbor in light
Worriedly demanded for the gem he claimed was lost
I apologized and cast a wistful glance despite
Handing it back, without any cost.

He looked amazed at my surrender
I told him that I knowingly trusted him so
He handed it back, from my polish still tender
Said I deserved the diamond aglow.

Today, I still cherish that tender start
To a friendship that seized me in its thrall
Even acquainted with his relatives in part
Such was the charm of this unexpected windfall.

A Snowy Night

Chilly winds nip at the ankles of frosted trees,
Blistering snow piles at the corners of the world,
An empowering silence blankets the night,
Whispering peace to a heart frayed by noise.
The white cloak of snow, gentle as memory,
Soothes the unrested, quieting the storm within.
Stars twinkle above, flickering like small torches—
Yet none compare to the moon, a circle carved in the sky.
It bathes the quiet world in light,
Pausing everything for a moment's perfect example,
Of how nature calms the overwhelmed,
Creating a fleeting peace we've learned to value.

Beyond the Story

Sinister sense of calm alluring,
A siren tugging me to my doom,
Engulfing me with tension palpable,
Air heavy, stone cold to the touch.

Suffocating my curiosity with suspense,
Flooding me with emotions raw and deep,
Leaving me straying to the edge of my seat,
And embracing the feelings as if they were mine.

Then comes the moment when all else is drowned out,
The climax, the height of the tale unbelievable,
Weaving a snare, an illusion irresistible,
Such that I question whether I'm the one living the story.

I have never known such a potent gateway,
Such an unbelievably strong and vivid illusion,
Before I flipped through this remarkable item,
Sloppily propped up against a bookshelf.

Yet, as I soon realize, this isn't illusion,
But a truth, shifting and malleable,
Revealing the hidden world behind,
By casting a different light upon it.

The Art of Becoming

When the tender future's mine to shape,
What mold do I use to form it?
When I have tools to incise and scrape,
Into what masterpiece should I transform it?

A forest of dreams to plant and raise,
Unknown wishes waiting to be extracted,
Cast a hook of doubt into a sea of haze,
No one knows what pastime will be retracted.

A canvas to brush with shades and hues,
The blaze of passion, nurture and increase,
An ocean to paint with greens and blues,
Futile wandering to finally cease.

Brake the anchor wherever you find it,
Like battling in court using the sword of reason,
Weave a tapestry and masterfully bind it,
Fight against small acts of treason.

Sketch the world and find your place,
Tame all the feistiest lions around,
Or go beyond and chart out space,
Nothing else will matter once your hobby is found.

So, I'll leap into the unknown ahead,
With steady hands and heart aglow,
The path I choose is where I'll tread,
And in that journey, I will grow.

Holiday Fever

Waking up to the bells' faint ringing
The feisty group of carolers singing
Threads of lights, parents stringing
Tinsel hovers after brother's flinging.

Eve of Christmas, day of cheer
The highlight of Santa's career
Children hoping for him to appear
Dressing up in holiday gear.

The infamous choice of naughty or nice
Saint Nick deliberately checking twice
Evolved from simple oranges and rice
To giving out gifts without a price.

Tidy up the house, hang a striped stocking
Ready the chimney for when Santa comes knocking
Prepare flimsy traps, spend the day clocking
All for when the reindeer come flocking.

As midnight strikes, the magic flows
Whispers of joy as the fireplace glows
Families gather where warmth bestows
Together in love, as the holiday grows.

Every Drop, Every Step

Recycle metal, paper, and plastic,
Preserve the Earth that slips from our grasp.
Take small steps, nothing too drastic—
Yet the planet's future is within our clasp.

Give plants and trees the care they deserve,
Be proud of the world you help sustain.
Show the planet that you, too, preserve—
Protect its life, its endless refrain.

Conserve water, use it with care,
Sustain the life that we live today.
Every drop counts, so let's be aware—
A cleaner world starts with the steps we take.

Springtime Symphonies

Trees wake, buds unfurling like whispered dreams
The sky a canvas of blue, brighter than it seems
Bird eggs slowly crack, life begins it cycle anew
A gentle sight indeed, a frail vision come true.

Golden daffodils gracefully stretch, reaching for the sun
Violets blush below them, their vibrant colors softly
spun
Yellow and blue—an artist's brushstroke ever so bold
Made into a symphony of spring, a ravishing story told.

Fragile rain falls like silver threads from the sky
Washing away winter's blissful and weary sigh
Each little drop a promise, each tiny splash a cure
A song of gradual renewal, steady and pure.

Flowers lithely sway, like dancers in a breeze
Petals twirling with grace beneath the trees
They leap and twirl in sudden bursts of light
A celebration of life, so luminous and bright.

But in this soothing dance, we must be wise
For nature's heart carries many skies
We must tend with a gentle, soothing care
So her eternal beauty lasts, beyond any compare.

Springtime whispers soft and true
In her every bloom, in her every hue
Let us listen, let us understand
We are the stewards of this land.

Whispers of the Wild

Creatures strewn, wild and free,
Darling, please come along with me!
Look at the peacocks, with their painted sails,
Spread their wings like colorful tales.

Underneath skies that softly sigh,
The leaves dance as small breezes fly,
Some birds, with beaks so long,
Sing their melodies, sweet and strong.

Lizards cling to sunlit stones,
Climbing life with silent tones,
And rabbits leap with paws that hum,
Weaving through fields, never numb.

The world around us breathes in rhyme,
A dance of nature and eternal time,
From creatures born of land and air,
To the fleeting moments, pure and rare.

Through valleys deep and mountains high,
We'll roam together, you and I,
With hearts unbound, and spirits free,
In nature's arms, we will always be.

Eternal Light

A burning ball of fire ablaze
Born from but a speck of debris.
This fiery wonder, invoker of praise,
Though frightening to a respectable degree.

Oh, scorching sun, giver of life,
We long for you when winter's cold descends.
Oh, gorgeous beauty, remover of strife,
We weep for you when summer's warmth ends.

Smoldering one, just out of our reach,
Distant friend never directly seen,
We seek your presence, humbly beseech,
When you are gone for periods unforeseen.

We need you, great one, effortlessly daunting,
There are many modeled after your tireless might,
But nothing matches your flaunting might,
And none can compare to your boundless light.

Oh, eternal sun, our constant guide,
Through endless cycles, your light we chase.
A brilliant force we cannot deny,
Yet in your warmth, we find our place.

Silent Moon

A silver orb in the midnight sky
A quiet glow that softly sighs
No fiery blaze, no searing gaze
Yet in its light, the world finds a quiet haze.

Oh, gentle moon, your guise we sketch
In every phase, it is silence we etch
You guide us through the darkest night
A constant in the endless flight.

No heat you give, no warmth to be seen
But still, you soothe us with tender sheen
A distant dream that pulls us near
A soothing comfort for every fear.

You wander high, so far from our reach
A silent guide, beyond our conceited speech
Your colors, a mystery to behold
In silver light, the night unfolds.

Oh, steadfast moon, serene and calm
In your embrace, we find our balm
While suns may burn with fierce delight
You offer peace in quiet light.

Overshadowed

"Stars are known for shifting across the sky," she said.
My future is uncertain, just like those specks.

"But they can't stray too far . . . you know why?"
I used to know, mother dear, but now I don't.

"Tell me, ma, please tell me!" I pleaded.
But what would be the use of pleading now?

"You see, my dear, they can't leave the moon."
You weren't supposed to leave me, either!

"They might enter another's territory," she explained.
You entered the heavens. You have no right to talk.

"And those beings might just snatch the stars away."
And here I am, left behind with only shadows.

She smirked as she caught me. "Like this!"
Oh, how I wish you were still here.

She added, "But they can't come too close, either."
I've grown to know that at a terrible cost.

"Why, mother?" I asked innocently.
Have I lost the innocence you left me with?

"See, those who come too close are overshadowed."
You brought them to us . . .

"They simply can't live in the shadow of the moon."
You didn't live, either.

"There needs to be a balance between the two."
As I said, no right to talk!

She points up from her place on the hill.
The same hill where you are right now.

"Always stay there, child. You'll be okay."
Well, guess what? I'm not!

"Overshadowed, yet still bathed in light . . ."
My eyes well up with water.

"Of course!" I tell her cheerfully. She smiles.
The tears flow down my face.

"Let's go inside, it's getting late."
I tremble, tears staining my face.

She gently tucks me in.
If only you could be here to do that now.

"Good night, my dear."
Good night, mother.

www.ingramcontent.com/pod-product-compliance
Lightning Source LLC
La Vergne TN
LVHW021306200726
843509LV00012B/1802